D1824422

One Hundred Years
OF HERITAGE
1903-2003
A history of State museums and heritage sites in Malta

KENNETH GAMBIN

HERITAGE BOOKS

IN ASSOCIATION WITH

H Heritage Malta

2003

ACKNOWLEDGEMENTS

In writing a book, even if a short one, one is bound to need the help and assistance of many persons. I am not going to mention them all but I would like to thank particularly Heritage Malta Chairman Dr Mario Tabone and the Chief Executive Officer Ms Antoinette Caruana for approving the idea of the exhibition and for their continuous help and encouragement to all those involved in its setting up, including the present booklet.

A word of thanks must also go to all members of the scientific committee, namely Mr Pierre Bonello, Mr Antonio Espinosa Rodriguez, Mr John J. Borg, and Ms Suzannah Depasquale for their help in making the dream project come true. I also have to thank all the curatorial and general staff of Heritage Malta for commenting on earlier versions of this booklet and suggesting several improvements, especially Mr Antonio Espinosa Rodriguez, who also indicated a number of interesting information and references. Thanks are also due to Mr Reuben Grima and Mr Nathaniel Cutajar for their valuable comments and suggestions. However, I take responsibility for all views expressed. Any errors of interpretation are obviously my own.

I must also thank Mr Pierre Bonello for his constant close cooperation and for the design of the display layout and Mr Charles Bonello, Mr Charles Borg, Mr Tony D'Amato, Mr Tonio Taliana, Mr Mario Coleiro, and Mr Anthony Damato for their technical support in mounting the exhibition.

Insight Heritage Guides Series No: 2
General Editor: Louis J. Scerri

Published by Heritage Books in association with Heritage Malta

Photo Credits
Unless otherwise stated all illustrations in this book are the property of the photographic archives of Heritage Malta.

Daniel Cilia, pages 4, 9, 12, 34, 35, 36, 37, 38, 39
Department of Information, pages 29, 31, 33

List of abbreviations

MAR	Museum Annual Report
NAM	National Archives of Malta
RWGD	Report on the Working of Government Departments
Ibid.	In the same place

ISBN: 99932-39-76-3

LIST OF CONTENTS

To all those,

who throughout the years

worked towards the conservation

and enhancement

of Malta's cultural heritage

PREFACE

The celebration of one hundred years of public curatorial history comes at a few months from when the structures established by our forefathers have been consolidated by new legislation. This legislation reflects the evolution in the administrative set up and reaffirms the priorities, which we as a nation should give our cultural heritage.

Since the days when the Museums Department was first established, the socio-economic life of the Islands have taken dimensions which were not anticipated by our forefathers. 'One Hundred Years of Heritage' succinctly delineates an evolution in the development of local museology, archaeological excavation and the keen interest in tracing our nations' origins. It is thanks to the ventures of Maltese pioneers like Sir Themistocles Zammit and Cavalier Vincenzo Bonello that we have become aware of our rich context. This publication is an essential historical delineation, which will guide us to manage our cultural heritage with the indispensable tools, ethics and hindsight.

Heritage as a concept has been evolving gradually not only through the contributions of Giovanni Francesco Abela, but also through the development of myths, legends and traditions. This is another form of historical narrative and documentation, which left an indelible mark on the *forma mentis*, character and life style of the Maltese. It is an intangible heritage, which reflects strong roots and a very sophisticated form of nationhood.

The traditions established by our predecessors and the development of popular historical narrative are today being supplemented by international norms, conventions and directives which Malta is adhering to and actively promoting. This publication is a valid contribution to the build-up of our consciousness vis-à-vis heritage.

Hon. Jesmond Mugliett B.E. & A (Hons.) A.& C.E.
Minister for Youths, Culture and the Arts

INTRODUCTION

Man is woven within the very fabric of history. As W. H. Auden put it, 'Man is a history-making creature who can neither repeat his past nor leave it behind'. And a society unmindful of its past risks not only the loss of its identity but also invites an uncertain future. A people without a proper understanding and appreciation of its past is culturally and psychologically handicapped, unable to attain social cohesion, political stability and a degree of greatness consistent with its dignity and self-esteem. Marcel Proust reminds us that: 'The past not merely is not fugitive, it remains present'. If a people is to move forward and meet ever new challenges, it must never forsake its roots; in a " Letter to a German", Jose Ortega Y Gasset warned: 'To excel the past we must not allow ourselves to lose contact with it; on the contrary, we must feel it under our feet because we raised ourselves upon it'.

That is why it is fit and proper to salute and remember the early pioneers of Maltese museology, beginning with Giovanni Francesco Abela, Agius de Soldanis, Fr Emmanuel Magri and the redoubtable Dr Temi Zammit and the other personalities that followed, so deftly chronicled in this booklet by Kenneth Gambin. They had the imagination, tenacity and vision to recover our collective past and present it as best they could, given the level of scholarship and science available to them. If we have wider horizons, we owe it to them; as Newton said: 'If I have seen further, it is by standing on the shoulders of giants'. In a literal sense, theirs was a historical task. They were conscious of their mission; what they were studying and researching was not only interesting in itself, intellectually, but provided the bedrock for national awakening. The Maltese archipelago may appear as specks in a wide sea, like thousands of islands dotting the seas and oceans; but they have a unique, lush and variegated heritage, the result of being, for millennia, a key geographical node in a constantly mutating and turbulent historical tapestry.

Museums not only deal with the past; they have an intriguing past themselves, as can be glimpsed in this booklet. Their story is intimately linked with social evolution in all its complex features-political realities, standards of education, economic factors, social classes and a more ineffable aspect: how a society looks at itself. Collections very often started as 'cabinets of curiosities', in the 17th and 18th centuries, when the world suddenly became larger, more accessible and enlightened minds were fired by the urge to know and discover. Of course, there were great collections in classical times and the Renaissance (like the Medici's) but these were more a matter of prestige and a display of power than a genuine attempt at understanding. When Peter the Great, who was driven by an insatiable passion to overtake the West in progress, asked Leibniz in 1708 what he should collect, the answer was revealing and amounted to practically everything: 'Such a cabinet should contain all significant things and rarities created by nature and man. Particularly needed are stones, metals, minerals, wild plants and their artificial copies, animals both stuffed and preserved ... Foreign works to be acquired should include diverse books, instruments, curiosities and rarities. In short all that could enlighten and please the eye'. One can appreciate how far modern museology has moved away from this idea of a freakish, though piquant, hodgepodge. Even Catherine the Great (Peter's daughter-in-law and herself a great collector) warned him that he could not 'enclose Nature in a cabinet - even a huge palace could not hold Her'. It is interesting that when Robert Darwin (Charles' great-grandfather) gave an account of 'a skeleton impressed in stone', he won an honorary mention in the Royal Society's Philosophical Transactions as a 'Person of Curiosity' (1719).

What may be termed the philosophy of museology has, of course, changed radically. Even as early as the last quarter of the 18th century, Giuseppe Benvicenni Pelli (the second director of the Uffizi) conceived the museum not as 'a monster of opulence' but 'as a useful depository for the conservation and spread of culture'. An acquaintance with the history of the 'museum', as this booklet provides, enriches one's experience. Annamaria Petrioli Tofani, writing about the history of the Uffizi, remarks: 'It is equally important that this history be known, at least in its general development, to those visiting the museum, in order that their experience go beyond the level of a casual encounter and become an intellectual and cultural event valued to the fullest in its significance and potential'.

The modern museum is no more a mere junk-shop cluttered with curios and odd 'antiquities'; of such, G. K. Chesterton lamented: 'It is meant for the mere slave of a routine of self-education to stuff himself with every sort of incongruous intellectual food in one indigestible meal'. The modern museum is conceived by experts, in a deliberate manner, to provide a space with a judicious selection of exhibits in order to offer a deep and meaningful experience to the visitor. The aim of a museologist is to make every visit not a casual one; even the aesthetics of the design is intended to create an area of silence and reflection, where the visitor confronts history, ingenuity and beauty. This goes beyond pedagogy - it is a fundamental human experience of the potential greatness and mystery of man; it amounts to an inner awakening, cultural and spiritual. Besides, every great museum is a window on the world; it is not just a 'national' museum. By its very nature, history connects and networks with other peoples, cultures, eras. A museum can be universal, though national, because history is intrinsically, though tangled, one kaleidoscope: 'History, with all her volumes vast, hath but one page'.

Heritage Malta has been mandated by Law (Cultural Heritage Act 2002) to be the national agency for museums and cultural heritage. It has the will and the vision to be worthy of public trust; it is building up the structure, the intellectual resources and the strategic plans to conserve and present, in the best possible way, our cultural heritage. No doubt, it is a mammoth task; this country is jam-packed with pre-historic and historic assets that make it into a great, little country. We owe it to us and to the world to inscribe cultural heritage among the top priorities of the national agenda; this would not only testify to how 'civilised' we are but would be a major economic player. It is imperative that Government and the people wake up to a grave and painful reality; our heritage is in crisis and degrading at an alarming rate. As a people, we have to invest heavily, in thought and financial means, in Heritage. We have to assure a future for our past; we have to be the guarantors of our collective memory. The past defines our identity and spells our future.

It is with a sense of anxiety that I hope, to paraphrase Kant, that we do not only live in an age of enlightenment but that we will be an enlightened age.

Dr Mario Tabone
Chairman - Heritage Malta

THE ORIGINS: GIOVANNI FRANCESCO ABELA

The origins of Maltese museology can be traced back to the first half of the seventeenth century, when Giovanni Francesco Abela (1582-1655), the Maltese vice-chancellor of the Order of St John, started collecting memorabilia regarding Maltese history and archaeology in his country house on a promontory overlooking the inner part of the Grand Harbour in Marsa. This villa, which he called *Museo di San Giacomo*, was built between 1628 and 1631, and was accessible both by land and sea. It followed the pattern of the cabinets of curiosities which were common in Italy and elsewhere, and to which visitors were occasionally admitted.[1] Most probably Abela's collection of antiquities was greatly influenced by that of the Bolognese Ulisse Aldrovandi. Abela in fact obtained a doctorate in civil and canon law in 1607, when Aldrovandi's collection was at the height of its fame.[2] According to Thomas Bartolin, a traveller from Copenhagen who visited Abela's museum in 1664,[3] the artefacts were attractively exhibited in various parts of the building. In the garden around the house, one could see statues, inscribed tablets, and marble fragments of ancient monuments. The museum itself, housed on the first floor, was reached through an impressive arched doorway which led into a central yard dominated by an obelisk. In it were displayed glass phials, decorated earthenware, sepulchral pottery, bones, medals, and bronze statuettes, among other things. Most of the artefacts were classified according to their provenance. It appears therefore that Abela's museum was more than simply a random assemblage of curiosities; it was somewhat well ordered. Among the imported objects he had some Etruscan and Greek pottery and Egyptian amulets. The most significant of the Maltese artefacts were the marble statue of Hercules, and a large collection of Greek and Roman coins.[4]

Typically, at a time when the word museum encompassed a variety of ideas, images, and institutions characteristic of the encyclopaedic tendencies of the age,[5] Abela's collection also included a number of fictitious objects pertaining to the world of myth and imagination. To Abela and his contemporaries, however, they proved the direct relationship that the Maltese islands had with the stories described in the Old and New Testaments and justified the imaginary stories which one could read in contemporary literature. Abela, therefore, had a political-intellectual agenda. He was trying to convey the message that Malta had a worthy and ancient past which was also noble and, above all, Christian. And his work and vision persisted for three centuries.[6] His collection also was the nucleus around which the

Top: Portrait of Gio. Francesco Abela in the National Library.

Above: The villa of Abela in an 18th century lithograph by Berthwult.

Artefacts from Abela's museum as depicted in his *Descrittione di Malta*.

The frontispiece of Abela's *Descrittione di Malta* (1647).

G.F. Agius de Soldanis (1712-70).

The marble statue of Hercules: one of the main artefacts in Abela's collection.

national collection subsequently grew and developed.

Through some passages in his major pioneering *Descrittione di Malta*,[7] one can also sense Abela's concern that heritage should in some way be regulated by the State. After his demise, the collection was bequeathed to the Jesuits, the main fount of higher education in Malta at that time. The deed of succession was actually signed in 1637, when Abela bequeathed the perpetual administration and usufruct of his country house, including the museum. The contract can now be found at the National Library. Some of the donated objects are actually listed. They included the marble statue of Hercules, eight gilt glass vases, three small glass vases with lids, fourteen gilt Murcia dishes, thirty-three frames (*quadretti*) with different curious figures, and four clay vases painted in red and black. The list continues with six small porcelain plates, twenty ordinary table plates in terracotta, one Egyptian mummy head, one branch of unworked coral, one tusk of a small elephant (two *palmi* long), and various small idols, oil lamps, and small perfume bottles found in ancient tombs.

One of the objects overlooked in the contract, and certainly one of the most important, was the sarcophagus discovered in Għar Barka, in the limits of Rabat, which is described in detail and illustrated in his book, even if it is probably different from the

one present in the collection today.[8] It is probable that some of the objects displayed in Abela's museum were of quite a recent origin.

By donating his collection to the Jesuit fathers, Abela probably was trying to put his collection in a safe and educational context where it would have been appreciated and improved. After all it was the Jesuit Order which, in the seventeenth century, first suggested innovative models in which to fit the new flow of knowledge 'within a traditional yet flexible framework'.[9] In fact one of the conditions of the deed made by Abela was that the collection should be rendered accessible to all interested scholars.

At first the Jesuits transformed Abela's residence into a place of retreat for members of their company and the museum was thus well catered for. In the first half of the eighteenth century, however, it was left to decay, especially when it was transferred to the residence of the knight Balì Francesco de Sousa in Għajn Dwieli, from where even some depredations were reported to have taken place, allegedly by French knights. In 1745 this sorry state of affairs prompted Canon Giovanni P. Francesco Agius de Soldanis (1712-70), the first librarian of the National Library who had seen the complete collection on many previous occasions, to comment that Abela

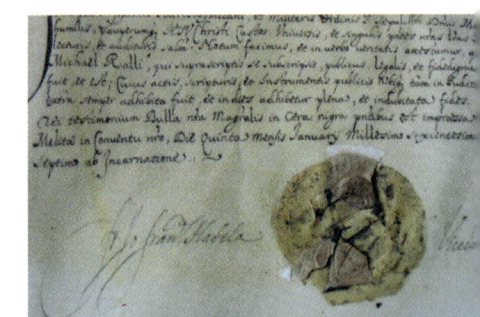

would have burst into tears if he could see the neglect in which his collection was to be found.[10] Twenty-three years later, in 1768, the surviving parts of the collection found their way into the hands of the Order of St John when, following similar developments in other European countries, the Jesuits were expelled from Malta by Grand Master Emanuel Pinto (1741-73). It appears that the objects were more appreciated in the Order's hands. However, members of the Order of St John seem to have been interested in antiquities only as far as their economic or aesthetic value was concerned. During the sixteenth century, for instance, several grand masters issued licences for the search of hidden treasures to the Maltese elite.[11] There appears to be no evidence that any attempt was made to recover any object for its historical and cultural value. Most of the remaining artefacts of Abela's collection were housed in the magisterial palace, the auberges of the knights, and, later, in a cabinet for the preservation of local antiquities in the new library in Valletta, constructed during the magistracy of Grand Master Emanuel de Rohan (1775-97). The actual transfer of Abela's collection to the library, however, did not take place before 1811, after instructions by Sir Hildebrand Oakes, the British commissioner of Malta (1810-13). The main aim was to

unire in un luogo solo, luogo pubblico e facile all'accesso di tutti, sien nazionali, sieno stranieri tutti quei monumenti d'antichita che si posson rinvenire in queste isole. Il luogo ella sa che e il nuovo edificio destinato alla libreria pubblica, ove ... saran collocati tutti i monumenti antichi che si trovano qui, compresi quelli che rinvengonsi nel Palazzo del Governo, e quelli altresi di cui alcun particolare vorra recarsi ad onore di farle un donativo.[12]

Some donations had already been made. In 1808, for instance, Gerolamo Ratto had donated *'un camelo, un lupo, un cinghiale ed un gatto selvatico in atto di sbranare un daino'* to the Public Library, *'per esser quivi conservate esposti all'osservazione d'ognuno'.*[13]

PRECURSORS AND EARLY DEVELOPMENTS

When the 'Grand Tour of Europe' became fashionable for the sons of the nobility or the rich, mainly from northern Europe, to complete their education, Malta became an increasingly attractive place to visit. Such 'cultural tourism', especially after the siege of 1565 and the building of Valletta, boosted the island's reputation as the bulwark of Christian Europe. Malta's frontier position, its increasing economic prosperity, and heterogeneous environment around the harbour area were also crucial factors in increasing this awareness. This resulted in an increased influx of travellers interested in the islands and their cultural and folkloristic heritage. Providentially, many of them had the habit of keeping detailed diaries which are a precious source of information about the whereabouts of Abela's collection and its use.

In 1787, for instance, when Jean Pierre Louis Houel (1735-1813), the engraver to Louis XVI, published the account of his voyages in the Mediterranean,[14] the four Roman bas-reliefs lay in one of the corridors of the palace, while previously they had been fixed as a decorative element onto the fountain in the main courtyard of the palace.[15] Other descriptions of the library-museum are not lacking. During his visit to Malta in 1797, the Norwegian traveller Peder Pavels and the Danish sculptor Bertel Thorvaldsen were shown around the *Bibliotheca* by the librarian, Abate Gioacchino Navarro, and were impressed by the 'considerable collection of Greek and Roman coins from various periods, mostly well preserved, a fine collection of recent medals in gold and silver, several hundred specimens of lava, a Hercules

Two of the paintings of Brockdorff depicting Maltese temples.

statue in white marble, several fine petrifacts some curious pieces of pottery from Antiquity, and the like'.[16] The magisterial palace also included a very large collection of paintings, furniture, and precious items, commissioned by various grand masters to commemorate special events or personalities, which had accumulated through the ages and adorned the various rooms of the palace.

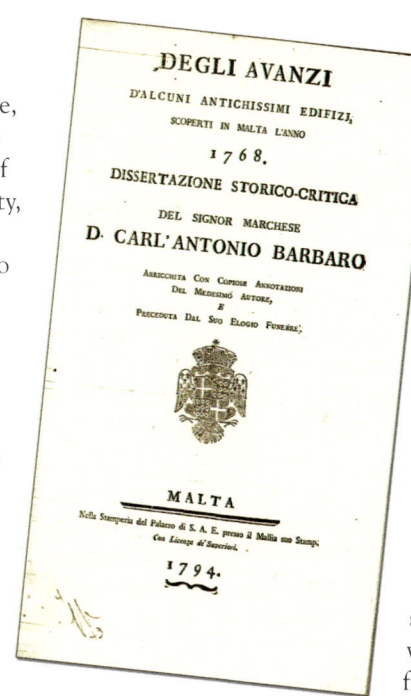

It appears that the artefacts were moved around frequently according to the different tastes of the different individuals responsible for them. According to Giuseppe Pericciouli Borzesi, who in 1830 published the *Historical Guide to the island of Malta and its dependence*, the four above-mentioned bas-reliefs were among other antique valuable articles preserved in the library, while eight years later George P. Badger recounts how 'in the same room with the library is also kept a small collection of antiquities and curiosities found at various times in the island, together with a few birds, a wolf, a wild cat and a snake, all stuffed'.[17]

Other local individuals also took a private interest in Malta's cultural heritage and started collections of their own. Marquis Testaferrata had a 'museum' in his palace at Marnisi, in the limits of Żejtun, while Marquis Carlo Antonio Barbaro hosted a permanent exhibition of antiquities in his residence opposite the Jesuit church in Merchants Street in

Valletta, which was even open for public viewing.[18] Most probably the bulk of Barbaro's collection came from the remains of some ancient structures which were discovered in Marsa, and about which Barbaro also wrote a report to Grand Master de Rohan.[19] Another subsequent collector was Canon Grech from Gozo, who met the German traveller Prince Herman Pückler-Muskau while on his visit to Gozo in 1835. According to the prince, Grech excavated his own fields and 'found so many antiques that he now had his own collection. Particularly noteworthy is a large quantity of glass vessels of all shapes and sizes, all in perfect condition'. His collection also included 'a large Phoenician copper medal … and two rare Corinthian coins of great beauty. Earthenware of all different types filled more cupboards, but none were decorated'.[20] However, apart from these private collections and the revision of G.F. Abela's *magnum opus* by Count Giovanni Antonio Ciantar (1696-1778) in 1772-80,[21] no major development occurred until the publications of Louis de Boisgelin[22] and Onorato Bres[23] (1763-1818) in the early nineteenth century.

A very important development which took place in the first half of the nineteenth century was that the study of antiquities ceased to be an exclusive hobby of aristocrats. British

The frontispiece of Carlo Barbaro's report on the finds at Marsa in 1794 (*centre*) and that of *Malta Antica* of Onorato Bres in 1816 (*below*).

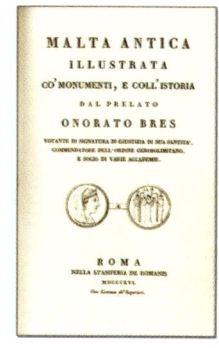

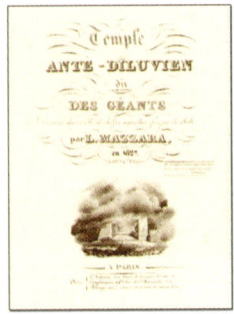

Mazzara's book on the temples of Malta published in 1827.

A showcase with Phoenician remains at the *Gabinetto delle Antichità*.

One of the earliest photographs of Ħaġar Qim before the restoration of the facade.

'arçhaeologists' and other travellers, artists, and military officers started showing interest in Maltese prehistoric remains and were granted permission to start excavating these sites. John Otto Bayer, commander of Gozo, together with Gozo's magistrate James Somerville, dug into the Xagħra Stone Circle and cleared Ġgantija in 1826-27, while Col. J.G. Vance, with the financial assistance of the British governor, Sir Henry Bouverie (1836-43), cleared Ħaġar Qim and Mnajdra in 1839-40.[24] No adequate records were kept of these clearing operations, and the most useful help comes from the drawings and watercolours by Charles Frederick von Brockdorff, who pictured the sites examined by Bayer. The British government for the first time even tried to purchase the site of the Xagħra Stone Circle but no agreement was reached on the price and the deal was not concluded. Other pioneers in this field were L. Mazzara, who published a brief description of the temples in Paris in 1827, and a similarly brief note by Captain William Henry Smyth in the journal *Archaeologia*, published by the

Society of Antiquaries in 1829.[25] Most of the material retrieved from these excavations was immediately lost, but some ended up filling various government departments. The majority of the latter, however, were deposited in the *Bibliotheca*, which slowly developed into a major collection since all librarians such as Gioacchino Navarro, Fr Bellanti, Dr

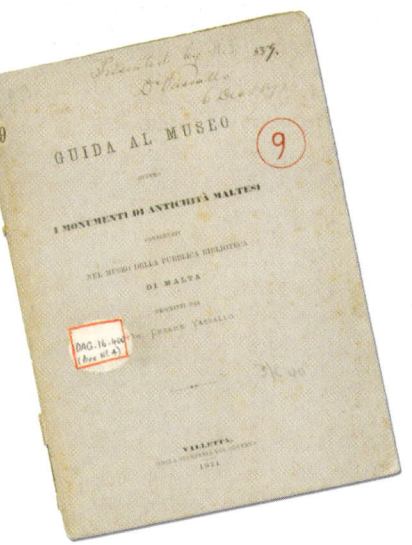

Cesare Vassallo, A.A. Caruana, and Filippo Vassallo, all continued to add objects which were discovered in Malta from time to time. The section of the library were this collection was housed was referred to as the *Gabinetto delle Antichità*. In it were displayed various clay and glass vases, sarcophagi, statues, inscriptions, and around 5,500 coins. The British governor Sir William Reid (1851-58) organized the collection in the inner two rooms of the library, thus drawing a line between the library and the museum, and in 1871 its 'curator' Dr Cesare Vassallo, who was also the librarian, published a guide book to help the visitor appreciate better the exhibits of what was perhaps the first real attempt at creating a national museum in Malta.[26]

In the meantime the British government intended to remove the collection of arms at the Palace Armoury for safe-keeping to London. Quantities of armour had already been shipped away during the troubled two-year French occupation and the early years of British rule. However, London's intention was never fully undertaken. Unfortunately this was a most travailed period for Malta's cultural heritage, resulting from the insensitivity of the British military rulers which resulted in the dismembering of Maltese cultural heritage from its natural regional context and inserting it instead into an alien colonial one. Among other things, they sold paintings from the Palace in public auctions since 'there were too much', poured boiling water on other paintings 'to clean them', awarded many pieces of armour to members of their families and friends as souvenirs, and sent cannon to London, from where, however, they were repatriated after a fierce patriotic campaign in the newspapers by Fortunato Mizzi.[27] In 1850 the Armoury was emptied to make room for modern British weapons, but five years later these new arms were removed by Governor William Reid (1851-58) as part of a rehabilitation plan, and a grand staircase was constructed as a public entrance. In 1857, a final attempt to remove the more important pieces to England failed. Under the direction of Governor Sir Gaspard Le Marchant (1858-64), armour was recovered from where it long lay abandoned and was duly cleaned and rearranged in the Armoury and palace corridors. In 1860 the Armoury was officially opened as Malta's first public museum.[28] This important event was followed five years later by another equally indicative development: the setting up of a Society of Archaeology, History and Natural Sciences of Malta, 'to preserve monuments and to encourage a taste for local archaeology and the natural sciences'.[29] Interest in cultural matters was slowly increasing.

In 1881 a formal request by the secretary of state for the colonies regarding the state of the temples

The Armoury in the late nineteenth century

Right: The first guide of the 'national collection' housed at the National Library by Dr Cesare Vassallo in 1871.

The title-page of one of the many books on the archaeological discoveries in Malta by A. A. Caruana

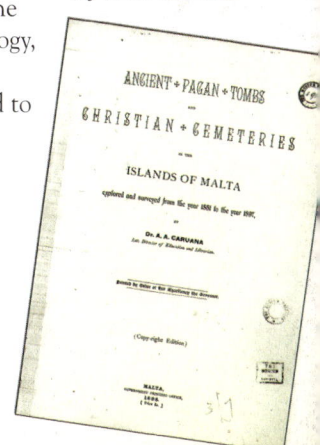

The brochure on the collection at the Public Library written by A. A. Caruana in 1898.

A Roman statue and the Cippus exhibited in the Bibliotheca in the late 19th century.

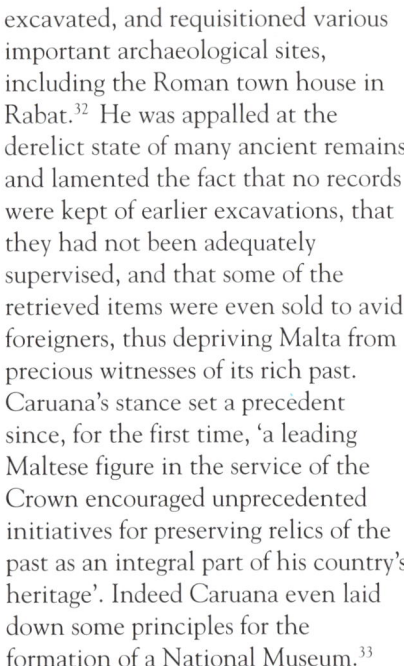

in Malta pushed Antonio Annetto Caruana, the director of education and curator of the collection of antiquities preserved at the Public Library, to publish a report on the archaeological antiquities in Malta,[30] which he later followed with other publications.[31] Caruana was entrusted with the archaeological explorations and preservation of local antiquities from 1880 to 1896. By then the forceful acquisition of archaeological sites by the government to protect public interest had become normal. In the process these sites were disembedded from the physical landscape and the local social fabric. Through cooperation with the superintendent of public works, Caruana discovered,

excavated, and requisitioned various important archaeological sites, including the Roman town house in Rabat.[32] He was appalled at the derelict state of many ancient remains and lamented the fact that no records were kept of earlier excavations, that they had not been adequately supervised, and that some of the retrieved items were even sold to avid foreigners, thus depriving Malta from precious witnesses of its rich past. Caruana's stance set a precedent since, for the first time, 'a leading Maltese figure in the service of the Crown encouraged unprecedented initiatives for preserving relics of the past as an integral part of his country's heritage'. Indeed Caruana even laid down some principles for the formation of a National Museum.[33]

From the academic point of view, however, Caruana was still enmeshed in proving the antiquity of Christendom in Malta and he still considered the sites as Phoenician. It had to be the German scholar Albert Mayr (1868-1924) who, in the last decade of the nineteenth century and the first decade of the twentieth century, through his objective analysis and publications,[34] at last interpreted the evidence gathered from the sites holistically, and demonstrated that they were much older and different from that of the Phoenicians and any other known Mediterranean culture.

Britain had no official government policy to establish museums in its colonies. It was left to the colonies to take the initiative. In fact the concept of public museum is essentially European in origin and it spread to other parts of the world through trading and colonial influence.[35] Even in Malta interest in heritage increased also as a result of colonial influence. Various British governors started showing interest in Malta's heritage, especially in its archaeological, military, and fine arts history. In 1888 Blanch Lintorn Simmons, daughter of Governor Sir John Lintorn Simmons (1884-88), catalogued all the State-owned dispersed collection of pictures. Her work, which was later published in a book,[36] was praised by the Maltese members of the Council of Government, namely by Dr Fortunato Mizzi, at a time of increasing Maltese political consciousness and a slowly but constantly growing sense of national identity, especially by the upper classes, following the birth of political parties.

The 'pressure' for some kind of cultural institution was increasing. A letter by John Henry Cooke in *The Malta Times and United Service Gazette* of 24 July 1891, for instance, was entitled 'Wanted – A Museum for Malta'. Parts of it are worth reproducing: *Museums constitute an important if not principal factor in the education of the people… The material that the island afford for the study of the natural and civil history of the central Mediterranean is practically unlimited … yet, save the work that has been undertaken by a few foreign enthusiasts and by one or two enlightened natives … no interest whatever has been or is evinced in the matter. It is a significant fact that while most of the principal museums of Europe possess some relic or*

other bearing on the former history of these islands … in Malta such treasures are not only regarded with indifference, but when found, they are absolutely neglected and are allowed to be either dispersed into the collections of private individuals, and foreign museums, or else they are relegated to some unsavoury room … It is a standing reproach against the people of Malta that they should possess so little of national pride as to allow such a state of things to exist. Malta requires a Museum. Why has she not one? … Such an institution is not a luxury; it is a necessity … The idea that a museum is simply a store house of curiosities has long since been discarded.[37]

Another development took place at the turn of the century in 1902, when Governor Lord Grenfell (1899-1903) engaged Guy Francis Laking, a renowned authority on arms and armour and keeper of the king's armoury, to properly classify, catalogue, and rearrange the collection of arms at the Palace Armoury. Laking separated the finer pieces from the rest, reorganized the display in a more pleasing manner, and also published a catalogue of the collection in 1903.[38]

John Cooke's letter in the press in 1891 exhorting the establishment of a national museum.

The marble statue of Hercules at the *Gabinetto delle Antichità*.

The title page of the seminal study on Maltese prehistory by the German scholar Albert Mayr.

DR THEMISTOCLES ZAMMIT
AND THE ESTABLISHMENT OF THE MUSEUM - 1903

The official ceremony of the opening of the grand exhibition in 1901.

Lieutenant Governor Sir Edward Merewether, the first chairman of the committee of management of The Museum.

A situation developed, therefore, where a number of Maltese individuals were reacting to British colonial interests and needs. While acting within government official channels, however, they were also taking some personal initiatives in a sector which was as yet unregulated by the State.

These two parallel forces finally resulted in a grand exhibition on Maltese antiquity being organized to coincide with the royal visit of the duke and duchess of York to Malta in 1901. The exhibition was managed by Themistocles Zammit (1864-1935), a remarkably versatile man who was a doctor by profession and acquired an international reputation in the field of medical research, but also proved himself as an eminent archaeologist and prolific writer. For the organization of the exhibition, which was housed in the Industrial Hall of the headquarters of the Society of Arts, Manufactures, and Commerce,

located at Palazzo Xara in Valletta, just opposite St John's Co-Cathedral, Zammit made best use of all the artefacts at his disposal. It was a great success which created a lot of enthusiasm and which eventually proved to be a catalyst for the official setting up of a museum in 1903 under the direction of Zammit who was appointed curator and secretary of a committee of management of what was popularly referred to as The Museum.[39]

The first chairman of the committee was the Lieutenant Governor Sir E. Merewether. Besides Dr Zammit, the other members of the committee, appointed by the governor on 12 June 1903 were the superintendent of public works (ex officio); the director of education (ex officio); Judge P. Debono, LL.D; W. Casolani, Esq.; Mgr. Dean V. Vassallo, DD; Fr. Emanuel Magri, SJ; Dr A.A. Caruana; and Carlo Zimmermann Barbaro.[40]

The appointment of this committee constituted the veritable act of birth of the Museums Department, even if it was not yet known as such. The committee not only had to advise the government on matters regarding heritage, 'for which up to present nobody seemed to be responsible', but was also the actual management arm of the museum, holding executive powers and directly responsible to the governor. A *Museum Annual Report*, which included the main achievements and donations received by the museum and national developments in the heritage sector, also started being published as from 1904. All government departments were also instructed to direct all objects which could be of possible interest to the Museum, so that the various collections dispersed through the islands would be concentrated and appreciated in one place.[41]

Zammit acted quickly. In his opinion, although the importance of the collection 'was recognized both in former and in recent times, no serious attempt has ever been made to increase the collection or at least to arrange and classify the exhibits in a manner to satisfy the requirements of students and the general public'. The collection was described, numbered and removed from the Public Library to Palazzo Xara 'for want of better accommodation' even if, in Zammit's own words, 'most articles were unfortunately unlabelled and whatever labels were found were mostly loose or worm-eaten beyond the possibility of deciphering'.[42] He wanted to create an educational institution that would put the history of the Maltese islands on a sound factual and scientific footing, and systematically classified the displayed artefacts according to their chronological period and provenance.

This clear methodical and scientific approach constituted 'a veritable intellectual and visual revolution in heritage presentation' and meant a complete rupture with Gio. Francesco Abela's essentially humanistic vision of history.[43] Moreover, the predominance of Punic and Roman artefacts was superseded by the steady inflow of prehistoric remains deriving from Zammit's and Fr. Emanuel Magri's (1851-1906) incessant archaeological excavations. The

Sir Themistocles Zammit, the father of the Museums Department.

The duchess of York visiting the exhibition on Maltese antiquity of 1901.

A general view of the exhibition arrangement in Palazzo Xara.

The wide interest shown in the newly-created Museum, officially inaugurated on 24 May 1905 by the Lieutenant Governor Merewether, was proved by a constant flow of donations, especially from the more cultured members of the higher echelons of society. Unfortunately the great majority of the working classes, fully dedicated to earn their daily bread, were still totally unaware of the significance of these developments in the cultural heritage sector. However, the increasing popularity of the Museum is also evinced by the number of visitors: 3,805 visited the Museum during the first year. This figure increased to 5,255 in 1908-09 and to 9,257 by 1916,[44] even if we do not know how many of the latter were in fact locals. Its activity also continued unabated. The Ħal Saflieni Hypogeum as well as the Tarxien Temples, together with a considerable number of tombs, were excavated by Fr. Magri and Zammit on behalf of the Museum. Magri also contibuted greatly to the local cultural heritage scene through his pioneering studies on Maltese folklore.[45]

Excavation works in progress in 1915 at the Tarxien Temples.

One of the earliest photographs of the Ħal Saflieni Hypogeum shortly after excavation.

establishment of the Museum, in fact, coincided, and was perhaps also the result of, a time of extensive structural works such as house building, road-works, and ancillary services such as drainage, which led to a considerable number of heritage-related discoveries all over the islands.

THE VALLETTA MUSEUM

All the sites mentioned above yielded great amounts of material. This meant that Xara Palace, the first premises of the museum, was soon rendered inadequate owing to the accumulation of artefacts, especially related to archaeology and fine arts. In fact the excavation of these newly-discovered monuments constituted an important development since external sites increasingly started being added to the Museum's responsibilities. By 1908 the Ħal Saflieni Hypogeum and the Roman Town House were opened to the public, while St Paul's Catacombs were added in 1910.[46] In the same year, probably because of the need to distinguish between the museum in the capital city and the Roman Town House, which was also referred to as the Rabat Museum, the Museum started being called the Valletta Museum.

Following this quick succession of developments, the need was increasingly felt to put the heritage sector on a more sound footing. The last straw was provided by a Gozitan farmer who deliberately destroyed a Phoenician house discovered on his land since the government did not want to pay the exorbitant price which he had requested, to Zammit's bitter disappointment. Legislation was finally enacted by an Ordinance of 1910 published in a *Supplement to the Malta Government Gazette*, which made provision for the protection and preservation of monuments and other objects of local antiquarian or archaeological importance, officially referred to as 'The Protection of Antiquities Ordinance, 1910'. The Ordinance, signed by Governor Sir Leslie Rundle (1909-15), included movable as well as immovable objects,

The 1910 'Protection of Antiquities Ordinance'.

St Paul's Catacombs shortly after being opened to the general public in 1910.

provided the right of pre-emption and expropriation by the government, and regulated all exportation and excavations, which were made subject to permission.[47]

THE MUSEUMS DEPARTMENT AND
THE AUBERGE D'ITALIE

Vincenzo Bonello (1891-1969), first curator of Fine Arts.

The first curator of the natural history section: Giuseppe Despott (1878-1936).

Archaeological artefacts sent to the Wembley exhibition of 1924.

A general view of the archaeological section as displayed at the *Auberge d'Italie*.

Another very important event took place in 1922, when the museum transferred its headquarters to the *Auberge d'Italie* in Merchants Street, and was officially integrated in the Civil Service. The annual report, in fact, started being presented to the minister of public instruction, and not to the governor, as before, even if other occasions arose when the report was once more addressed to the governor according to the political vicissitudes of the island as the constitution was granted and withdrawn following the necessities of the British empire.

The department was divided in four sections. The director was Dr Temi Zammit, who was also the curator of the archaeology and history section. The arts section was headed by Vincenzo Bonello (1891-1969); the natural history division by Giuseppe Despott (1878-1936); and the mineralogical section by Dr Lewis Mizzi (1847-1935).[48] By 1924 all curators started to present an individual annual report, instead of a single one representing the entire work of the Museum. This ramification was a natural and beneficial development due to the growing collection and the increasing specialization following the growing array of interests. The arts section, for instance, set up a conservation laboratory for the restoration of paintings and other works of art, and the natural history section was able to receive a substantial donation previously housed at the University of Malta. Both sections also initiated a separate photographic collection.

Temporary exhibitions and seminars also started being organized regularly. Worthy of mention, for instance, is the participation in the Grand British Empire Exhibition, held at Wembley in 1924, for which a preliminary exhibition for the selection of the works of art and other exhibits to be sent to Wembley was organized at the

Auberge d'Italie. The interior of the Malta Pavilion, which externally had the appearance of a walled fortress, was made up of three large halls, one for the island's prehistory, another for Malta during the knights' period, and one for contemporary industry, trade, and art. According to *The Times* of London, by means of the exhibition in the pavilion, which also won first prize in a competition held for that purpose, Malta was 'able to convey a lasting impression … in which fifty centuries of history are faithfully represented'.[49] The pavilion was officially opened by Lord Grenfell, former governor of Malta, to who, in Temi Zammit's opinion, 'the Museum owns its present independent existence'.[50] Grenfell had indeed been instrumental for the issuing of the Government Notice of 1903 establishing the management committee for the museum, and he also gave a personal donation of Egyptian antiquities in order to be exhibited, among which was a complete Egyptian mummy presently stored at Vilhena Palace in Mdina.

The new Valletta museum was officially inaugurated one year later, on 19 November 1925, by Governor Sir Walter Congreve. According to Zammit, the museum was 'arranged so as to give the visitor a practical demonstration of the physical features of the Maltese Islands, their paleontological remains, their old and modern fauna, and the history of their inhabitants from the Stone

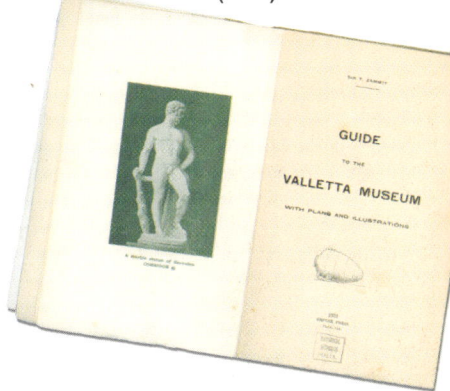

The title page of T. Zammit's *Guide to the Valletta Museum* (1931).

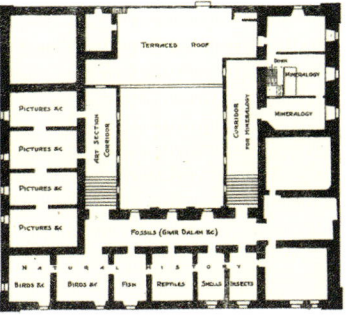

GROUND FLOOR

FIRST FLOOR

The general plan of the various sections as distributed in the *Auberge d'Italie*.

A general view of the historical section in the *Auberge d'Italie*.

23

The main staircase of the Inquisitor's Palace during restoration works by Vincenzo Bonello in the late 1920s.

The first of the five issues of the Bulletin of the Museum, issued in 1929.

Age period to the present day'.[51] All the work being carried out by the Museums Department was also given further legal strength with the *Antiquities Protection Act*,[52] which was once more brought about by a hotly debated 'act', when the Franciscan friars demolished the oratory, sacristy, and part of their convent in Valletta. The aim of the law was 'to amend and consolidate the laws relating to the protection of antiquities', namely the Ordinance of 1910. A significant change regarded the antiquities committee, which was now reduced to a consultative role to the governor on matters relating to cultural heritage, and had no role whatsoever in the management of museums and sites.

The work of the museums department continued in full swing. The Inquisitor's Palace in Vittoriosa was added to the list of sites managed by the department, and in 1927 a

course on general archaeology by Temi Zammit at the *Auberge d'Italie* was very well attended.[53] Starting from December 1929, five issues of the *Museum Bulletin*,[54] which included scholarly contributions by the curators of the museum, were also published. According to its editor, Temi Zammit, 'the growing importance of the Valletta Museum has moved the government to sanction the periodical publication of a Bulletin … to enhance the practical value of the museum'.[55] Zammit also published various editions of guide books for practically all the archaeological sites in Malta, including the Valletta Museum.[56] The confidence of the general public in the museum and its reputation grew increasingly and this was reflected with a constant flow of donations, among which one has to mention those of Dr Lewis Mizzi, Dr E. Parnis, Mrs Zammit Clapp, Francesco They, Prof. S.L. Pisani, G. Muscat Azzopardi, and Capt. Olaf Gollcher.

Other museums and sites were also opened to the public. Both Mnajdra and Ħaġar Qim were made accessible free of charge to all those who wanted to visit them. As a consequence of transport problems, however, few availed themselves of this opportunity, since the sites were so far away. They started drawing considerable numbers from the mid-1930s onwards following the increasing popularity of motor cars, presumably owned by the more well-to-do and educated sectors of society who could afford such a luxury.[57] Another development concerned Għar Dalam, where a series of large-scale excavations were carried out by John H. Cooke, Giuseppe Despott, Carmel Rizzo, and Joseph Baldacchino between 1892 and 1937. The large amounts of organic remains

Themistocles Zammit, with his camera, during an on site inspection at Ta' Ħaġrat Temples in June 1926. *Left:* The covers of Zammit's guide books to various Museums Department sites.

unearthed from the cave created a huge storage problem and in 1930 a small museum was built to house it. The cave was also opened to the public in 1933.[58] The activity and good work of the museums department also led the Museums Association of London, in the same year, to include Malta's museums in a specialized book on the subject, which included a general description and basic information on all the museums in Malta.[59]

The museums department suffered a setback with the death of Sir

Themistocles Zammit in 1935. In the words of Carmel Rizzo, his successor as director of the department, 'Sir Temi Zammit was to all practical purposes the founder of the Museum of Malta, and it is entirely due to his great and untiring activity that the museum has attained its present great scientific and historical importance both locally and abroad.'[60] According to Hannibal Scicluna, eventually also acting-director of the museums department, Zammit was a 'uomo di vario ingegno e di grande intelligenza, dotato per giunta di una robusta costituzione e di una attività prodigiosa'.[61] Unfortunately his death was also soon followed by those of Giuseppe Despott and Lewis Mizzi, two pioneers of the study of natural history and former curators. The museum thus lost three out of four curators in one year, closely followed by the death of Temi Zammit's successor, Carmel Rizzo, in 1938. Hannibal Scicluna was appointed acting director in his stead.

Top: Dr Lewis Mizzi (1847-1935), the donor of his extensive mineralogical collection to the Museum and the first mineralogical curator of the Museums Department.

Above and left: Għar Dalam before being completely excavated.

FROM THE SECOND WORLD WAR
TO THE NATIONAL MUSEUM

Potentially the Second World War could have been a period of great discovery in Malta since excavations and quarrying were conducted on an unprecedented scale owing to its inhabitants' desperate search to provide safe underground shelter against enemy bombing. However, as the newly-appointed director of the department, Joseph Baldacchino, pointed out in 1947, regrettably 'relatively few finds came to the notice of the Museum, and presumably many discoveries in archaeology and geology must have passed unnoticed and unrecorded'.[62] But other priorities were at stake, and the work of the museum was completely disrupted by the outbreak of the Second World War. All sites which had been open to the public had to be closed, with the exception of St Paul's Catacombs, which remained accessible. The cave of Għar Dalam was first forced into by refugees and used as an air-raid shelter and later even requisitioned by the military authorities as a fuel storage depot, while the Inquisitor's Palace, which also went through some very close shaves, was given to the Dominican fathers to use as a convent and church, since theirs, a few metres away from the palace, had been completely destroyed.[63] The prehistoric temples of Kordin suffered extensive damage through war action. The same occured to the collections stored at the Auberge d'Italie, which went through two direct hits. The collection which fared worse was that of natural history, since it was kept in a wing of the building which was hit by the bombing. Other exhibits

War devastation: the remains of Palazzo Xara, which hosted the Museum from 1903 to 1922.

Malta's heritage suffered great losses during World War II.

Capt Charles Zammit, director of the Museums Department from 1955 to 1971.

Antonio Sciortino (1879-1947), curator of the fine arts section.

pertaining to the other sections had been removed first to the Public Library, then to a rock shelter in Mellieħa, where they suffered as a result of humidity and lack of ventilation, later to Verdala Palace, and subsequently to the inquisitor's summer residence at Girgenti, where most of the collection was still amassed in 1947.[64] Museum authorities paid frequent visits to these locations and gave advice in connection with the best possible conservation of the artefacts. The second hit, however, still damaged greatly the works of art which had been deposited at the auberge for safekeeping or for restoration by third parties, since the museums department was also entrusted with the preservation and safe custody of works of art existing in churches under government control, the governor's palace in Valletta, government departments, and even private collections, including church authorities. In fact the Roman Town House at Rabat, being distant from the main war action around the harbour area, started being used as a restoration laboratory.

After the war, the most urgent priority was to restore what had been damaged. In 1944 a committee, chaired by Charles Zammit, the son of Sir Themistocles Zammit, was appointed to survey and report on the condition of over 2,000 historic monuments.[65] Antonio Sciortino, the successor of Vincenzo Bonello as curator of the Fine Arts Section, did his utmost to recover whatever could be recovered.[66] Gradually the Museum resumed many of its normal activities and museums and sites slowly started re-opening their doors to the public. In April 1945, for instance, the Roman Town House was re-opened to the public, followed by Għar Dalam in 1947, and by the numismatic collection in the same year, which was exhibited once more in the same room where it was exhibited before the war. The number of donations slowly gathered pace once more, the most important certainly being the conchological collection of Giuseppe Mamo and the original plaster models of the statues of Antonio Sciortino upon his death in 1947.[67] In 1948 the Palace Armoury was officially handed over from the public works department to the museums department and added to the museums managed by the latter. It quickly became the most popular of all museums. The Ġgantija Temples were also opened for the first time to the public free of charge in 1948-49.[68] In 1950 an extremely popular exhibition commemorating the victorious outcome of the Great Siege of 1565 was also held at the Armoury, and in 1951 the Museum participated in an exhibition held at the Royal Malta Library to coincide with the visit of members of the World Organization of the Teaching Profession. In 1954 a small two-room museum was also set up at the Tarxien Temples in order 'to display and interpret the finds from the adjoining temples'. A similar museum was set up one year later at the Ħal Saflieni Hypogeum. In the words of David Trump, curator of archaeology between 1958 and 1963, in a matter of a few years and 'in the face of many difficulties, the museum has regained what it had lost and more'.[69]

But just when the department started finding its feet again, in 1954 it was forced out of the Auberge d'Italie to make room for the courts of justice, and a sample of the collections were squeezed uncomfortably at Casa Leone in Santa Venera, which was justly described as a 'token museum'.[70] Fortunately, however, this humiliating exile from the capital city did not last long and one year later, in 1955, the department acquired a new centre

from where to operate. After the necessary rehabilitation works, the Auberge de Provence in Republic Street, Valletta, which housed the administration section as well as the display of the archaeological and fine arts collections, was inaugurated on 11 January 1958 as the National Museum. In the previous year, as a foretaste of things to come, the two paintings of Caravaggio, *The Beheading of St John* and *St Jerome*, were exhibited at the Auberge de Provence after having been restored by the *Istituto Centrale del Restauro* of Rome. In eight months the two paintings were viewed by more than 11,000 people.[71]

The official inauguration of the National Museum at the *Auberge de Provence* in 1958.

General views of the mounting of *The Beheading of St John* and *St Jerome* at the *Auberge de Provence* in 1957. Visitors viewing the two masterpieces.

EXPANSION AND INCLUSION

Post-independence stamps depicting Malta's cultural heritage.

David Trump's arrangement of the archaeological collection in the late 1950s.

Reflecting European academic developments, since its establishment in 1903 the Museum has endeavoured to widen its scope. Gradually, especially following the progressive democratization of culture after the Second World War, a wider meaning started being given to the word 'heritage', which started moving away from an elitist mentality concentrating on rare artefacts of monetary value and to incorporate popular daily traditions, crafts, and oral culture. The result has been the gradual establishment of different museums covering a range of themes comprising geology, underwater archaeology, the fine arts, military and naval history, and ethnography and intangible cultural heritage.

This movement coincided also with the need for self-assertion and search for a national identity by the Maltese people after independence, especially after the colonial period, since local politics in the earlier part of the century between a Nationalist and an Imperialist party were fought basically on a largely cultural basis. Heritage, especially archaeological traditions, played an important role in this duel, since historical facts were thwarted in order to be used as part of political rhetoric, which 'availed of the past as a device of justification', and opposing 'political groups appropriated antique objects and archaeological sites in order to claim for themselves a distinct identity'.[72] After the Second World War it was increasingly realized that museums had a role to play in contributing to national consciousness, providing a sense of belonging to the Maltese people and preserving the nation's identity through its historic and cultural heritage. Heritage was also consciously used by the independent Maltese government as a symbolic tool through which to promote a precise identity of a young nation but with a millennial history. The most glaring example of this shift took place in philately: whereas in the colonial period all symbols which the Maltese could have identified themselves with, such as the temples, were relegated to very high values not used by the public, the exact contrary started taking place in the post-independence era, when cultural heritage symbols were pictured in

stamps with the lowest
denominations, and therefore with
the widest use and circulation.

New museums were opened during
the 1960s and 1970s as a consequence
of various factors coming from within
the museums department itself, as well
as a response to outside forces and
interests. First of all, the constantly
increasing specialization of the
collections and consequent lack of
necessary exhibition and storage space
necessitated new buildings to host
them. Some of the latter were
provided by the British military forces,
which left a number of sites empty
when they departed from the islands.
The State also felt the need to
increase adequate places of cultural
interest, since the demand for them
slowly increased, especially because
the Maltese economy was becoming
increasingly geared to the tourist
industry. At first museums were
considered simply as an added option
to the sun-and-sea-seeking tourists.
Later, however, with the increasing
emphasis on quality and cultural
tourism, they started being considered
as the main attraction of the islands.
The way forward in this regard was
already clear by 1964, when the
museums department hosted two
UNESCO experts who were in Malta
to 'investigate the part which
museums and monuments could play
in the tourist industry of Malta'.[73] The
number of people visiting museums in
Malta in fact continued to rise, mainly
owing to the increasing number of
tourists arriving every year.
Collaboration with foreign scholars,
set off by Temi Zammit in the early
twentieth century, resumed once more
after the war, a case in point being the
very important contribution given to
local archaeology by Prof. John Evans
and Dr David Trump in the 1950s and

1960s, who through their studies and
publications, enabled a more precise
sub-division of the different cultural
phases of Maltese prehistory.[74]

Gozo opened its first museum in
Casa Bondì at the Citadel on 30 May
1960, where various artefacts related to
the island's history previously kept at
the Gozo Public Library or displayed in
Malta were exhibited.[75] The
Inquisitor's Palace in Vittoriosa was
made accessible to the public free of
charge in 1967. In the same year
official plans were once more made by
the government for the Auberge
d'Italie to revert back to the
department and be used as the
National Archaeological Museum once
the building was vacated by the law
courts. A detailed report was prepared
by Prof. Franco Minissi, an Italian
architect of international fame in
museum buildings, on the
rehabilitation of the building to host 'a
general re-organization and expansion
of the main function of the
Archaeological Section, i.e. display,
conservation, and storage material,
study collections and educational

**Prime Minister,
George Borg Olivier
during the official
inauguration of the
Gozo Museum in
1960.**

**Part of the facade of
Casa Bondi in the
Citadel, Gozo, which
presently houses the
Archaeological
Museum of Gozo.**

Minister A. Barbara, during the inauguration of the National Museum of Natural History at Vilhena Palace, Mdina (*top*).

services'. By 1970 most of the library had already been transferred to the auberge and classified. In 1971, however, a re-assessment of public office accommodation in Valletta led to the assignment of the former Admiralty House to the department to host the future museum of fine arts in substitution of the Auberge d'Italie.[76] The museum of archaeology, therefore, remained at the Auberge de Provence.

Unfortunately in 1971 it was decided that there were no funds for the publication of the *Museum Annual Report*. A very brief report was instead included in the general report submitted by all government departments. However, activity continued unabated. The National Museum of Natural History, whose collection was left stored in boxes after the ravages of the war for lack of space, was inaugurated at Palazzo Vilhena, Mdina in 1973. It included the collections of geological specimens, fossils, animal skeletal anatomy, fishes, insects, birds, and land and sea shells.[77] The fine arts collection departed from the National Museum at the Auberge de Provence, which was left solely for the exhibition of the increasing archaeological collection and was thus re-christened National Museum of Archaeology. The fine arts collection

was transferred to the Admiralty House, Valletta, where it was officially inaugurated as the National Museum of Fine Arts in 1974. It immediately became the foremost organizer of temporary exhibitions in the Maltese islands, especially of contemporary works of art both by Maltese and foreign artists, thus making a significant contribution to cultural activity in Malta.[78] Following an unfortunate political decision the Armoury was transferred from its original location to the ground floor of the grand master's palace in 1975.[79] Following this setback, however, the department quickly recovered with other successes. The National War Museum followed closely after. It was set up also through the efforts of dedicated enthusiasts, founders of the National War Museum Association, and was inaugurated in a wing of Fort St Elmo in 1976, after a highly successful exhibition of relics of the First and Second World Wars was held there in the previous year.[80] Both Ħaġar Qim and Mnajdra temples also officially opened their doors once again to the public free of charge in 1977,[81] closely followed by the State Rooms and Tapestry Chambers in the palace in 1979.[82]

The 1980s were not less busy for the museums department. The year 1981

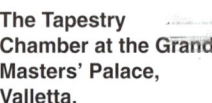

The Tapestry Chamber at the Grand Masters' Palace, Valletta.

saw the opening of the National Museum of Folklore in a section of the Inquisitor's Palace, and a National Museum of Political History in the Auberge de France in Vittoriosa.[83] A complementary museum to the Folklore Museum was also inaugurated in the Citadel, Gozo in 1983.[84] The latter allowed Casa Bondì, which had been used as a general museum on Gozo since 1960, to be dedicated exclusively to archaeology, and in fact it was inaugurated as such in 1986.[85] Both the Children's Museum and the Museum of Contemporary Art,[86] even if short-lived, pointed the way forward for the museums department to be more inclusive both in the nature of the exhibits as well as new audiences which had to be catered for. The opening of all the above-mentioned museums was no mean feat, especially when one considers that the majority are housed in buildings which were not built specifically as museums. Mostly are seventeenth- and eighteenth-century palaces, which are in themselves of great historical,

architectural, and cultural value. Frequently, in fact, the history of the building itself tends to impinge on the particular nature of the exhibits and the collection is closely related to the building in which it is housed. Historical buildings present a specific challenge, since they had to be converted into museums while respecting as far as possible the particular fabric of the edifices concerned, especially when introducing modern day amenities necessary to render a building relevant for today's society, such as new electrical systems, lifts, and access for the disabled.

At the same time a policy of change and upgrade initiatives was adopted in response to evolving political realities, changing social concerns, new scientific discoveries, and public contributions. In the first place the department increasingly participated in international exhibitions, such as the exhibition on the Order of St John at Versailles in 1961, and the organization of the XIII International

Archbishop Michael Gonzi during the inauguration of the National Museum of Fine Arts in 1974.

General views of the National Museum of Fine Arts when the museum practically included everything which was not archaeological.

One of the showcases in the 'Roman Villa' in the early twentieth century, when emphasis was on quantity rather than quality.

'Malta a Maritime Nation': an exhibition held at the Malta Maritime Museum in 2003.

Council of Europe Art Exhibition on 'The Order of St John in Malta' at the State Rooms of the palace and at St John's Museum in 1970.[87]

Throughout a century of existence, museum philosophy has witnessed a number of developments following growing concern about the effectiveness of museum communication. Besides the traditional lectures, a breakthrough in communication methods was made in 1960 when Dr David Trump, the curator of archaeology, gave a series of six interviews on Rediffusion describing the island's prehistory, while members of staff of the National Museum of Fine Arts helped to produce art programmes which were transmitted on the State television station.[88]

Display also underwent a revolution. In general terms, the first phase was distinguished by a desire to collect for the sake of impressing through the sheer quantity of exhibits, which generally ended up displayed on top of each other. During the second stage a sequence was given to the exhibited items by displaying them in a chronological order. This meant that there was a definite path which one had to follow in order to be able to understand the meaning of the display. The last development was characterized by a desire to inform and to share an experience. This was achieved by shifting the focus from one concentrated on quantity to one of quality, by means of which one could better interpret, demonstrate, and explain a particular point or concept. In this way the visitor is not forced to follow a particular trail, but could roam freely about at his pleasure without missing the whole message. Where necessary, a link with the particular sites was provided through photographs and multi-media presentations. Special attention was also dedicated to the text accompanying the exhibits, which was also a development in itself.

Apart from the informative aspect, a complementary development was the increasing importance being given to design and display. The museums department passed from the use of wooden showcases before the Second World War, to 'Edmund' brass showcases in the 1950s, and finally to heavy investment in international standard highly sophisticated and climate-controlled showcases in the 1990s. The same can be said of lighting concepts. General lighting by means of neon tubes was abandoned in favour of a low-voltage halogen ultra-violet protection system and lately even fibre-optic, thus also giving greater importance to conservation concerns. The great effort given to these aspects of museology is also reflected in the fact that as from the late 1980s the museums department started employing designers who are now adequately equipped to produce all necessary material in-house, thus ensuring uniformity.

The work of the museums department received further international recognition when in 1980 two sites, namely the Ħal Saflieni Hypogeum and Ġgantija temples, were inscribed in the UNESCO World Heritage List, being considered to 'bear a unique or at least exceptional testimony to a cultural tradition or to a civilization which is living or which has disappeared'. In 1992 this was extended to five other prehistoric temple sites: Ħaġar Qim, Mnajdra, Tarxien, Skorba, and Ta' Ħaġrat.[89]

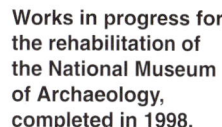

Another wave of museums were opened in the 1990s, including the Museum of Natural Science at the Citadel, Gozo, in 1991, and the Ta' Kola Windmill in Xagħra, Gozo, and the Malta Maritime Museum in the former Naval Bakery in Vittoriosa in 1992.[90] In the same year the ethnography section was also introduced in the Museums Department to cater for popular traditions and values, which were somewhat discarded in favour of more traditional subjects. The Old Prisons in the Citadel, Gozo were opened to the public for the first time in 1996. Two years later saw the opening of the refurbished display of the National Museum of Archaeology, while the ultra-modern conservation project and new visitor centre of the Ħal Saflieni Hypogeum was inaugurated in 2000.

The state-of-the-art Hypogeum project inaugurated in 2000.

Works in progress for the rehabilitation of the National Museum of Archaeology, completed in 1998.

RECENT DEVELOPMENTS

An important internal development took place in 1996, when the administrative section of the museums department was for the first time separated from the archaeological section. Moreover, in 1996 the first draft law proposing to reform the museums department was also proposed in the House of Parliament by minister for justice and culture, Dr Michael Refalo. But the law did not make it through the preliminary discussion process since it was automatically rendered obsolete after the holding of general elections and consequent change of government in the same year. The new minister for education and national culture, Mr Evarist Bartolo, had to start anew, but there was yet another change in government in 1998 and unfortunately there was not enough time for his efforts to bear fruit.

The long-proposed and awaited major structural change of the museums department finally took place in 2002, when minister for education and culture, Dr Louis Galea, with the cooperation of both sides of the House of Parliament, finally updated the 1925 legislation on the protection of antiquities to reflect modern realities by the Cultural Heritage Act,[91] whose purpose is 'to make provision in place of the Antiquities Protection Act for the superintendence, conservation and management of cultural heritage in Malta'. By means of this new legislation the Museums Department ceased to exist and three new institutions were created in its place, namely a Superintendence of Cultural Heritage, with a regulatory function of the heritage sector, Heritage Malta, the national operations agency of the government of Malta in charge of museums, sites and collections, and a Committee of Guarantee to ensure the collaboration between the different agencies and advise government on the national strategy for the protection and management of cultural heritage. The Cultural Heritage Act also included the recently established Malta Centre for Restauration which offers a degree in conservation studies in collaboration with the University of Malta. This new set-up ensures a very solid basis for the cultural heritage sector in Malta on which to plan for the necessary future development.

Heritage Malta commenced operations on 1 January 2003. It is the veritable successor of the museums department, taking over the majority of personnel previously employed by department and entrusted with the management, conservation, interpretation, and marketing of all national museums and heritage sites, as well as their related collections in Malta and Gozo. It is acting as a champion for education and outreach programmes, providing physical and intellectual access to all, and generating economic and tourism potential. On 25 September 2003, Heritage Malta inaugurated its new head office premises in a wing of the Old University Building, the former College built by the Jesuits in the new city of Valletta in 1595, transformed into a university by Grand Master Pinto in 1769, and partly used as the first Lyceum in Malta in 1833.

The frontispiece of the Cultural Heritage Act (Malta) 2002, which reformed the cultural heritage sector in Malta.

The official logos of Heritage Malta, The Superintendence of Cultural Heritage and Malta Centre for Restoration.

The new offices of Heritage Malta.

FROM THE PAST TOWARDS THE FUTURE

The need for this structural reform had long been felt and needed since the previous legal set-up and chronic lack of necessary human and financial resources did not allow the museums department to fully develop all its potential. The department constantly sought to broaden its operations by combining museum functions with other cultural and social activities, while ensuring that it provides an ever-increasing range of services, including public lectures and seminars, libraries and publications, events and social activities, and temporary and international exhibitions.[92] All this was also made possible through external financial aid and grants, or expert advice, from special sources such as the Getty Foundation, the World Monuments Fund, UNESCO, ICOM, and ICOMOS, together with the support of various 'Friends of the Museum' associations. Invaluable help was also received from volunteer groups and individuals, and from experience through collaboration with non-governmental organizations and the local and foreign universities, among which one has to mention the *Missione Archeologica Italiana*, which has enriched our knowledge through its archaeological research in Malta in collaboration with the department during the last forty years. Contact with foreign institutions, especially by means of participation in conferences and seminars abroad, has also allowed the department to keep up to date with the latest conservation and restoration techniques. More than anything else, however, one has to pay tribute to the dedicated service of all the staff of the

museums department who through the years, in one way or another, contributed towards the department's considerable achievements. Theirs was a sterling service which often went beyond their normal duties but which they nonetheless carried out owing to their unwavering dedication and wholehearted commitment to their nation's heritage, and which more often than not was taken for granted and consequently not even recognized.

It has been a century of achievement in education, research and interpretation, development and dissemination of knowledge, service, conservation, restoration, contribution to the tourist industry, safeguarding our cultural heritage, and, therefore, our national identity, for future generations. Heritage Malta has now been empowered to build on the foundations which have been laid before.

Through Heritage Malta, museums are now being integrated more strongly with the community and play an increasingly important educational role in creating awareness on the social value of cultural heritage. Instead of merely reflecting the history of Maltese society, museums are now playing an active role in shaping it.

Groups of visitors flocking to heritage sites and seeking to enrich their experience of Malta.

The brochure of the archaeological exhibition held in San Marino, 2001.

Prime Minister Edward Fenech Adami visiting the archaeological exhibition set up in Prague in 1999.

APPENDIX I – Chronology of Museums and Heritage Sites

1. Palace Armoury – 1860 (Museums Department in 1951)
2. The Museum, Palazzo Xara – 1903
3. St Paul's Catacombs – opened to public in 1911
4. Valletta Museum – 1910
5. Roman Town House – Discovered 1881 and opened to the public in 1911 and in 1983
6. The Valletta Museum (Auberge d'Italie) – 1922
7. Tarxien Temples – Discovered in 1913; first excavated in 1915, opened to public in 1932
8. Għar Dalam Cave and Museum – 1930 and 1933, 1950, 2002
9. Ġgantija Temples – First mentioned in the 18th century; first excavated in 1827, opened to the public in 1949
10. The National Museum, Auberge de Provence – 1958
11. Hal Saflieni Hypogeum – Discovered in 1902, opened to the public in 1911 and 2000
12. Gozo Museum – 1960
13. Inquisitor's Palace – 1967
14. National Museum of Natural History – 1973
15. National Museum of Fine Arts – 1974
16. National War Museum – 1976
17. Lascaris War Rooms – 1986

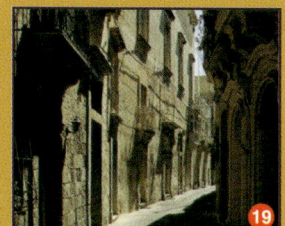

18. State Rooms and Tapestry Chambers – 1979

19. National Museum of Political History – 1981

20. National Museum of Folklore – 1981

21. Museum of Folklore, Gozo – 1983, 1985

22. Museum of Archaeology, Gozo – 1986

23. Armoury, Gozo – 1984

24. Museum of Contemporary Art – 1986

25. Children's Museum – 1987

26. Natural Science Museum, Gozo – 1987 and 1991

27. Malta Maritime Museum – 1992

28. Ta' Kola Windmill, Xagħra, Gozo – 1992

29. Gozo Old Prisons – 1996

30. National Museum of Archaeology – 1974 and 1998

31. Ħaġar Qim Temples – First mentioned in the 17th century; first excavated in 1839; opened to the public in 1977

32. Mnajdra Temples – First excavated in 1840

33. Roman Baths, Għajn Tuffieħa – Discovered in 1929

34. Skorba Temples – Discovered in 1914; first excavated in 1961

35. Ta' Ħaġrat Temples – Discovered in 1916; first excavated in 1923

36. San Pawl Milqi Roman Villa – Discovered in 1963, opened to the public in 1990

37. Borġ in-Nadur – First excavated in 1881

MALTA

GOZO

Comino

St. Paul's Bay

Mellieħa

Gharghur

Naxxar

Mosta

Lija

Balzan

Birkirkara

San Gwann

Gżira

Sliema

Valletta

Floriana

Msida

Hamrun

Marsa

Attard

Qormi

Żebbuġ

Siġġiewi

Dingli

Rabat

Mdina

Paola

Fgura

Tarxien

Santa Luċia

Luqa

Għaxaq

Gudja

Mqabba

Kirkop

Safi

Qrendi

Żurrieq

Żejtun

Marsaxlokk

Birżebbuġa

Marsascala

Żabbar

Cospicua

Senglea

Vittoriosa

Għarb

Żebbuġ

Marsalforn

Xagħra

Victoria

Kerċem

Sannat

Nadur

Qala

Mġarr

Għajnsielem

Xewkija

APPENDIX II – Directors of the Museums Department

Prof. Sir Themistocles Zammit	*(1922-35)*
Cav. Vincenzo Bonello	Acting Director *(1932)*
Carmel Rizzo	*(1935-38)*
Prof. R.V. Galea	Acting Director *(1938)*
Chev. Hannibal P. Scicluna	Acting Director *(1938-47)*
Chev. Dr Joseph G. Baldacchino	*(1947-55)*
Capt. Charles G. Zammit	*(1955-71)*
Dr John A. Cauchi	Acting Director *(1967)*
Francis S. Mallia	*(1971-81)*
Fr Marius Zerafa, OP	*(1981-90)*
Dr Tancred Gouder	*(1990-97)*
Anthony Pace	*(1998-2002)*

APPENDIX III – Curators of Sections

The Museum
Dr Themistocles Zammit, Curator (1903-10)

The Valletta Museum
Dr Themistocles Zammit, Curator (1910-21)

Fine Arts
Cav. Vincenzo Bonello, Curator (1922-37)
Antonio Sciortino, Curator (1937-47)
Dr John A. Cauchi, Curator (1953-71)
Fr Marius Zerafa, OP, Assistant Curator and Curator (1970-81)
Dominic Cutajar, Assistant Curator (1988-90)
Antonio Espinosa Rodriguez, Assistant Curator (1988-90)
    *given duties at the Malta Maritime Museum
Dominic Cutajar, Curator (1990-2000)
Antonio Espinosa Rodriguez, Curator (1990-03)
    *1990-2001 given duties at the Malta Maritime Museum
Adrian Bartolo, Assistant Curator (1997-1999)
Theresa Vella and Dennis Vella, Officers in Charge (2000-02)
Antonio Espinosa Rodriguez, Curator (2002-03)

Archaeology
Sir Themistocles Zammit, Curator Archaeology [& Historical] (1922-34)
Capt. Charles G. Zammit, Acting Curator (1932)
Capt. Charles G. Zammit, Assistant Curator (1933-34)
Capt. Charles G. Zammit, Curator (1934-58)
Prof. R.V. Galea, Acting Curator (1938)
Dr Joseph G. Baldacchino, Acting Curator (1938-39, 1941-43)

Dr David Trump, Curator (1958-63)
Francis S. Mallia, Curator (1959-71)
Dott. Tancred Gouder, Assistant Curator (1970-75)
Francis S. Mallia, Acting Curator (1974-76)
Dott. Tancred Gouder, Curator (1975-90)
Anthony Pace, Assistant Curator (1990-91)
Anthony Pace, Curator (1991-97)
Nathaniel Cutajar, Assistant Curator (1992-97)
Reuben Grima, Assistant Curator (1992-97)
Anthony Pace, Chief Curator (1997-98)
Nathaniel Cutajar, Curator (1997-2002)
Reuben Grima, Curator (1997-2002)
Suzannah Depasquale, Assistant Curator (1997-2003)
Mark Anthony Mifsud, Assistant Curator (1997-2002)
Michelle Buhagiar, Assistant Curator (1997-2002)

Malta Maritime Museum
Antonio Espinosa Rodriguez, Assistant Curator (1988-90)
  * Curator of Fine Arts
Antonio Espinosa Rodriguez, Curator (1990-2003)
  * Curator of Fine Arts
Emmanuel Magro Conti, Assistant Curator (2000-03)

Ethnography
Dr Carmel Cassar, Curator (1992-98)
Kenneth Gambin, Officer in Charge (1998-2000)
Kenneth Gambin, Assistant Curator (2000-03)

Natural History
Giuseppe Despott, Curator (1922-33)
Dr Lewis Mizzi, Curator Mineral & Crystallographic Section (1922-35)
Dr Joseph G. Baldacchino, Curator (1933-47)
Dr Harry Micallef, Part-Time Curator (1966-70)
Dr Carmel De Lucca, Part-Time Assistant Curator
  Ornithology/Entomology (1967-71)
Dr George Zammit Maempel, Part-Time Assistant Curator Geology/
  Palaeontology and Ghar Dalam (1967-87)
Dr George Zammit Maempel, Part-Time Curator Geology/
  Palaeontology and Ghar Dalam (1988-2002)
Joseph Vella Gaffiero, O/Charge, Natural History Museum (1972-2000)
John J. Borg, O/Charge, Natural History Museum (2000-03)

Military History Unit
Stephen Spiteri, Acting Curator (1995-98)
Michael Stroud, Assistant Curator (1990-2003)

Gozo
George Azzopardi, Assistant Curator Archaeology (1998-2003)
  * Officer in Charge, Gozo Museums and Sites

APPENDIX IV –
Governors and Ministers responsible for cultural heritage

Lieut.-Gen. Lord Grenfell	Governor, 1899-1903
Gen. Sir Charles Mansfield Clark	Governor, 1903-07
Lieut.-Gen. Sir Henry Fane Grant	Governor, 1907-09
Gen. Sir Henry Macleod Leslie Rundle	Governor, 1909-15
F. Marsh. Lord Paul Sanford Methuen	Governor, 1915-19
F. Marsh. Lord Herbert Plumer	Governor, 1910-21
Mgr. Dr Francesco Ferris	Minister of Education, 1921-23
Can. Enrico Dandria	Minister of Education, 1923-24
Can. Enrico Dandria	Minister of Education and Emigration 1924-27
Prof. Augusto Bartolo	Minister of Education and Emigration 1927-30
Gen. Sir John Philip Du Cane	Governor, 1930-31
Gen. Sir David Graham Campbell	Governor, 1931-32
Mgr. Prof. Enrico Dandria	Minister of Education, 1932
Dr Enrico Mizzi	Minister of Education, 1932-33
Gen. Sir David Graham Campbell	Governor, 1933-35
Gen. Sir Charles Bonham Carter	Governor, 1935-40
Gen. Sir William Dobbie	Governor, 1940-42
F. Marsh. Viscount Gort	Governor, 1942-44
Lieut.-Gen. Sir Edmund Schreiber	Governor, 1944-46
Sir Francis Douglas	Governor, 1946-47
Dr Godwin G. Ganado	Minister of Education, 1947-50
Dr George Borg Olivier	Minister of Education, 1950-51
Dr Jackie Frendo Azzopardi	Minister of Education, 1951
Dr Fortunato Mizzi	Minister of Education, 1951-52
Dr Jackie Frendo Azzopardi	Minister of Education, 1952
Dr Carmelo Schembri	Minister of Education, 1952-53
Dr George Borg Olivier	Minister of Education, 1953-54
Dr Antonio Paris	Minister of Education, 1954
Ms Agatha Barbara	Minister of Education, 1955-58
Lieut.-Gen. Sir Robert Laycock	Governor, 1958-59
Admiral Sir Guy Grantham	Governor, 1959-62
Dr Antonio Paris	Minister of Education, 1962-66
Dr Paolo Borg Olivier	Minister of Education, Culture & Tourism, 1966-71
Ms Agatha Barbara	Minister of Education & Culture, 1971-76
Ms Agatha Barbara	Minister of Labour, Social Services & Culture, 1976-81
Dr Alex Sceberras Trigona	Minister of Foreign Affairs & Culture, 1981-87
Dr Ugo Mifsud Bonnici	Minister of Education, 1987-92

Dr Ugo Mifsud Bonnici	Minister of Education & Human Resources, 1992-94
Dr Michael Refalo	Minister for Youth & the Arts, 1994-95
Dr Michael Refalo	Minister of Justice & Culture, 1995-96
Mr Evarist Bartolo	Minister of Education & National Culture, 1996-98
Dr Louis Galea	Minister of Education, 1998-2003
Mr Jesmond Mugliett	Minister for Youth & the Arts, 2003-

APPENDIX V – Chairpersons Heritage Malta
Alexander Grech (2002-03)
Dr Mario Tabone (2003-)

BIBLIOGRAPHY

National Archives of Malta (Santo Spirito Hospital, Rabat), 'Letters from Office of the Public Secretary: 1 August 1808 – 15 April 1812'.

Abela, G.F., *Della descrittione di Malta isola nel Mare Siciliano* (Malta, 1647; facsimile edition Malta, 1984).

Abela, G.F. and Ciantar, G.A., *Malta Illustrata* (Malta, 1772-80).

Agius de Soldanis, G.P. Francesco, *Gozo. Ancient and Modern, Religious and Profane* (Malta, 2003). Translated by Anthony Mercieca.

Badger, G.P., *Description of Malta and Gozo* (Malta, 1838).

Barbaro, C.A., *Avanzi d'alcuni antichissimi edifizi scoperti in Malta l'anno 1768* (Malta, 1794).

Bonello, G., 'The Gozo megalithic sites: Early visitors and artists', in A. Pace, ed. (Malta, 1996), 19-29.

Bonello, G., 'Malta in the Wembley Exhibition, 1924', in *Histories of Malta II. Figments and Fragments* (Malta, 2001), 215-9.

Bonello, V., 'Quod non fecerunt barbari ...', *Malta Letteraria. Rassegna di Lettere, Scienze e Arti*, xi (Malta, 1914), 299-305.

Bonanno, A., 'Giovanni Francesco Abela's legacy to the Jesuit College', in *Proceedings of History Week 1983*, ed. M. Buhagiar (Malta, 1984), 27-37.

Bonnici Calì, R., 'The corner-stone of the Malta Museum', in *G.F. Abela* (Malta, 1961). 70-81.

Braun, H., *Works of art in Malta. Losses and survivals in the war* (London, 1946).

Bres, O., *Malta antica illustrata co' monumenti e coll'istoria* (Rome, 1816).

Bulletin of the Museum, i, 1-5 (Malta, 1929-35).

Caruana Galizia, D., 'Antonio Annetto Caruana: the incidental archaeologist' (BA Hons. dissertation, University of Malta, 1997).

Caruana, A.A., *A report on the Phoenician and Roman antiquities in the group of the islands of Malta* (Malta, 1882).

Caruana, A.A., *Ancient pagan tombs and Christian cemeteries explored and surveyed from the year 1881 to the year 1897* (Malta, 1898).

Caruana, A.A., *The Royal Public Library of Malta* (Malta, 1898).

Caruana, A.A., *Ancient pottery from the ancient pagan tombs and Christian cemeteries in the islands of Malta* (Malta, 1899).

Cassar, C., *Witchcraft, sorcery and the Inquisition. A study of cultural values in early modern Malta* (Malta, 1996).

Cooke, J.H., 'Wanted – A Museum for Malta', *The Malta Times and United Service Gazette*, 24 July 1891.

Cutajar, N., 'Origins of the National Museum of Archaeology', *Treasures of Malta*, ii, 1 (Christmas 1995), 67-71.

De Boisgelin, L., *Ancient and modern Malta* (London, 1804-05).

Directory of Museums and Art Galleries in British Africa and in Malta, Cyprus and Gibraltar (London, 1933).

Espinosa Rodriguez, A., 'The national museums: Origin and development', in *Heritage. An encyclopaedia of Maltese culture and civilisation*, iv, 1025-35.

Evans, J.D., *The prehistoric antiquities of the Maltese islands: a survey* (London, 1971).

Findlen, P., 'The Museum: Its Classical etymology and Renaissance genealogy', *Journal of the History of Collections*, i, 1(1989), 59-78.

Findlen, P., *Possessing nature. Museums, collecting and scientific culture in early modern Italy* (California, 1996).

Freller, T., 'Excavators and adventurers. The history of three bas-reliefs in the Museum of Archaeology', *Treasures of Malta*, ix, 2 (Easter 2003), 51-4.

Fsadni, M., *Id-Dumnikani Maltin fi zmien il-Gwerra 1939-1945* (Malta, 1977).

G.F. Abela: Essays in his honour by members of the Malta Historical Society (Malta, 1961).

Gouder, T., 'The progressive unveiling of Maltese prehistory', in A. Pace ed. (Malta, 1996), 13-8.

Houel, J., *Voyage pittoresque dans les isles de Sicile, Lipari et Malte* (Paris, 1782-87).

http://whc.unesco.org/criteria.htm

Laking, G.F., *Catalogue of the Armour and Arms in the Armoury of the Knights of St John of Jerusalem* (London, 1903).

Lewis, G., 'Museums and their precursors: a brief world survey', in J.M.A. Thompson (ed.), *Manual of Curatorship. A guide to museum practice* (London, 1984).

Mayr, A., *Die Vorgeschichtlichen Denkmäler von Malta* (Munich, 1901).

Mayr, A., *Die Insel Malta in Altertum* (Munich, 1909).

Mazzara, L., *Temple ante-diluvien dit des giants dans l'isle de Gozo* (Paris, 1827).

Mifsud Chircop, G., *Manwel Magri: Ħrejjef Missirijietna* (Malta, 1994)

Mizzi, P., 'The national museums: A historical background', *Heritage. An encyclopaedia of Maltese culture and civilisation*, iii, 868-75.

Museum Annual Reports 1903-1969.

Museum Revenue Book from 1905-1979.

Pace, A. (ed), *Maltese prehistoric art 5000 – 2500BC* (Malta, 1996).

Pericciuoli Borzesi, G., *Historical guide to the island of Malta and its dependence* (Malta, 1830).

Reports on the working of Government Departments 1970-2002.

Report on the working of the Museum Department for the year 1970 (Malta, 1972).

Scicluna, H., 'Temistocle Zammit', *Archivio Storico di Malta*, II, 7 (Rome, 1936), 1-4.

Simmons, B., *Description of the Governor's Palaces* (Malta 1888/95).

Smyth, W.H., 'Notice of some remains at Gozo, near Malta', *Archaeologia*, xxii (1829).

Sorensen, S. and J. Schirò (eds.), *Malta: 1796-1797. Thorvaldsen's visit based on the unpublished diary of Peder Pavels* (Malta, 1996).

Spiteri, S.C., *Armoury of the Knights. A study of the Palace Armoury, its collection, and the military storehouses of the Hospitaller Knights of the Order of St John* (Malta, 2003).

Stöger, H., 'Albert Mayr (1868-1924)', *Malta Archaeological Review*, No. 4 (Malta, 2000), 3-9.

The Malta Government Gazette (various issues).

Thompson, J.M.A., (ed.), *Manual of Curatorship. A guide to museum practice* (London, 1984).

Trump, D., 'The archaeological collections of the National Museum', *The Malta Year Book 1959*.

Trump, D., *Skorba* (London, 1966).

Vance, J.G., *Description of an ancient temple near Crendi, Malta* (Malta, 1840).

Vassallo, C., *Guida al Museo, ovvero i monumenti di antichità Maltesi conservati nel museo della pubblica Biblioteca di Malta* (Malta, 1871).

Vella, D., *Antonio Sciortino: Monuments and Public Sculpture* (Malta, 2000).

Vella, N., and O. Gilkes, 'The lure of the antique: Nationalism, politics and archaeology in British Malta (1880-1964), *Papers of the British School at Rome*, lxix (Oxford, 2001), 353-84.

Zammit, T., *Guide to the Valletta Museum with plans and illustrations* (Malta, 1931).

NOTES

1. G. Lewis, 'Museums and their precursors: a brief world survey', in J. M. A. Thompson (ed.), *Manual of curatorship. A guide to museum practice* (London, 1984), 9. See also P. Findlen, *Possessing nature. Museums, collecting and scientific culture in early modern Italy* (California, 1996).

2. Personal communication by Mr Rueben Grima.

3. T. Zammit, *Guide to the Valletta Museum* (Malta, 1931), 5.

4. P. Mizzi, 'The national museums: A historical background', *Heritage. An encyclopaedia of Maltese culture and civilisation*, iii, 868-75; R. Bonnici Calì, 'The corner-stone of the Malta Museum', in G. F. Abela: Essays in his honour by members of the Malta Historical Society (Malta, 1961), 70-81.

5. P. Findlen, 'The Museum: Its Classical etymology and Renaissance genealogy', *Journal of the History of Collections*, i, 1 (1989), 59.

6. N. Cutajar, 'Origins of the National Museum of Archaeology', *Treasures of Malta*, ii, 1 (Christmas, 1995), 67-71.

7. G. F. Abela, *Della descrittione di Malta isola nel Mare Siciliano* (Malta, 1647).

8. A. Bonanno, 'Giovanni Francesco Abela's legacy to the Jesuit College', in M. Buhagiar (ed.), *Proceedings of History Week 1983* (Malta, 1984), 27-37.

9. Findlen, 'The Museum', 66.

10. For a short review of the history of Abela's collection, see A.A. Caruana, *The Royal Public Library of Malta* (Malta, 1898), 15.

11. C. Cassar, *Witchcraft, sorcery and the Inquisition. A study of cultural values in early modern Malta* (Malta, 1996), 74.

12. NAM, Letters from Office of the Public Secretary: 1 August 1808 – 15 April 1812. Letter dated 31 January 1811, f. 189: 'collect in one public place, easily accessible to all foreigners as well as locals, all antique artefacts which can be found on these islands. As you know, the said place is the building of the public library … where all ancient objects which can be found here, including those which are to be found in the Governor's Palace and others which may be donated, will be located'. Reference kindly provided by Mr Antonio Espinosa Rodriguez.

13. Ibid. Letters dated 20 and 30 August 1808: 'a camel, a wolf, a boar and a wild cat in the act of attacking a deer … to be conserved and exhibited for all to see'. Reference kindly provided by Mr Antonio Espinosa Rodriguez.

14. J. Houel, *Voyage Pittoresque dans les Iles de Sicile, Lipari, et Malte* (Paris, 1782-87).

15. T. Freller, 'Excavators and adventurers. The history of three bas-reliefs in the Museum of Archaeology', *Treasures of Malta*, ix, 2 (Easter 2003), 51.

16. S. Sorensen and J. Schirò (eds.), *Malta: 1796-1797. Thorvaldsen's visit based on the unpublished diary of Peder Pavels* (Malta, 1996), 59.

17. G. P. Badger, *Description of Malta and Gozo* (Malta, 1838), 185.

18. Mizzi, 872.

19. C.A. Barbaro, *Avanzi d'alcuni antichissimi edifizi scoperti in Malta l'anno 1768* (Malta, 1794).

20. G. Bonello, 'The Gozo megalithic sites: Early visitors and artists', in A. Pace (ed.), *Maltese prehistoric art* (Malta, 1996), 21.

21. G. F. Abela and G.A. Ciantar, *Malta Illustrata* (Malta, 1772-80). One also has to mention 'Gozo. Ancient and Modern, Religious and Profane', written by Agius de Soldanis in 1746 but not published until the 20th century.

22. L. de Boisgelin, *Ancient and modern Malta* (London, 1804-05).

23. O. Bres, *Malta Antica* (Rome, 1816).

24. J.G. Vance, *Description of an ancient temple near Crendi, Malta* (Malta, 1840).

25. T. Gouder, 'The progressive unveiling of Maltese prehistory', in A. Pace (ed.), 14.

26. C. Vassallo, *Guida al Museo* (Malta, 1871).

27. V. Bonello, 'Quod non fecerunt barbari…', *Malta Letteraria. Rassegna di Lettere, Scienze e Arti*, xi (Malta, 1914), 299-305. Reference kindly provided by Mr Antonio Espinosa Rodriguez.

28. S. Spiteri, *Armoury of the Knights. A study of the Palace Armoury, its collection, and the military storehouses of the Hospitaller Knights of the Order of St John* (Malta, 2003), 201-28.

29. N. Vella and O. Gilkes, 'The lure of the antique: Nationalism, politics and archaeology in British Malta (1880-1964), *Papers of the British School at Rome*, lxix (Oxford, 2001), 354.

30. A.A. Caruana, *A report on the Phoenician and Roman antiquities in the group of the islands of Malta* (Malta, 1882).

31. A. A. Caruana, *Ancient pagan tombs and Christian cemeteries explored and surveyed from the year 1881 to the year 1897* (Malta, 1898), and *Ancient pottery from the ancient pagan tombs and Christian cemeteries in the islands of Malta* (Malta, 1899).

32. On A.A. Caruana, see D. Caruana Galizia, 'Antonio Annetto Caruana: the incidental archaeologist' (BA Hons. dissertation, University of Malta, 1997).

33. Vella and Gilkes, 355.

34. Foremost among his books are *Die Vorgeschichtlichen Denkmäler von Malta* (Munich, 1901) and *Die Insel Malta in Altertum* (Munich, 1909). See also 'A letter from Dr Albert Mayr to Sir

Themistocles Zammit re archaeological material from the Hypogeum' (1907), conserved in the library of the National Museum of Archaeology, Valletta. *Die Vorgeschichtlichen* was later translated into English for private circulation in 1908. On Mayr see H. Stoger, 'Albert Mayr (1868-1924)', *Malta Archaeological Review*, No. 4 (2000), 3-9.

35. Lewis, 12.

36. B. Simmons, *Description of the Governor's Palaces* (Malta, 1895).

37. J.H. Cooke, 'Wanted – A Museum for Malta', *The Malta Times and United Service Gazette*, 24 July 1891. Cooke was a teacher of English at the Valletta Lyceum and editor of the *Mediterranean Naturalist* (1891-93). He also carried out excavations at Għar Dalam (see below). Information kindly provided by Mr Antonio Espinosa Rodriguez and Mr John J. Borg.

38. G. Laking, *Catalogue of the armour and arms in the armoury of the Knights of St John of Jerusalem* (London, 1903).

39. For a short history of the Museums Department, see A. Espinosa Rodriguez, 'The national museums: Origin and development', *Heritage. An encyclopaedia of Maltese culture and civilization*, iv, 1025-6.

40. Government Notice No. 113, *Malta Government Gazette* No. 4599, 12 June 1903.

41. *Museum Annual Report 1903-04, Supplement to the Government Gazette* No.4747, 25 August 1904, i-iii.

42. Ibid.

43. Cutajar, 69-70.

44. *MAR 1905-06*, 4; *MAR 1908-09*, 4; *MAR 1915-16*, 10.

45. For a biography of Magri see G. Mifsud Chircop, *Manwel Magri: Ħrejjef Missirijietna* (Malta, 1994).

46. MAR *1907-08*, 9; *Museum Revenue Book from 1905-1979*.

47. Ordinance No. IV, *Supplement to the Malta Government Gazette*, 17 June 1910, 1-5.

48. *MAR 1922-23*, 1.

49. G. Bonello, 'Malta in the Wembley Exhibition, 1924', in *Histories of Malta II. Figments and Fragments* (Malta, 2001), 215-19.

50. *MAR 1903-04*, 2.

51. Zammit, 9.

52. 'Antiquities Protection Act', *Malta Government Gazette*, 27 July 1925.

53. *MAR 1928-29*, 1.

54. *Bulletin of the Museum*, i, 1-5 (Malta, 1929-35).

55. *MAR 1929-30*, 3.

56. These include *The Neolithic Temples of Hal Tarxien Malta* (1929), *The Neolithic Hypogeum at Hal Saflieni* (1935), *The Neolithic Temples of Hajar Kim and Mnaidra* (1927), *The St Paul's Catacombs* (1926), and *The Roman Villa Museum* (1930).

57. *MAR 1933-34*, 1.

58. *MAR 1932-33*, 1.

59. *Directory of Museums and Art Galleries in British Africa and in Malta, Cyprus and Gibraltar* (London, 1933).

60. MAR 1935-36, 1.

61. H. Scicluna, 'Temistocle Zammit', *Archivio Storico di Malta*, ii, 7 (Rome, 1936), 1: 'a man of various skills and great intelligence, gifted with a robust constitution and of prodigious activity'.

62. *MAR 1946-47*, 1.

63. M. Fsadni, *Id-Dumnikani Maltin fi żmien il-Gwerra 1939-1945* (Malta, 1977), 147-50.

64. *MAR 1946-47*, 9-10.

65. *MAR 1946-47*, 2-3.

66. This particular aspect of the work of Sciortino is presently being studied by Anthony Spagnol, one of the restorers of the National Museum of Fine Arts.

67. *MAR 1946-47*, 8; *MAR 1947-48*, 7. For a comprehensive study on Sciortino see D. Vella, *Antonio Sciortino: Monuments and Public Sculpture* (Malta, 2000).

68. *MAR 1948-49*, 4, 9.

69. D. Trump, 'The archaeological collections of the National Museum', *The Malta Year Book 1959*.

70. *MAR 1954-55*, 4-5; *MAR 1955-56*, 2, 8.

71. *MAR 1956-57*, 1; *MAR 1957-58*, 1, 11.

72. Vella and Gilkes, 353.

73. *MAR 1964*, 1.

74. See, for instance, D. Trump, *Skorba* (London, 1966) and J. Evans, *The prehistoric antiquities of the Maltese islands: a survey* (London, 1971).

75. *MAR 1959-60*, 1.

76. *MAR 1967*, 2-3; *MAR 1968*, 2; *RWGD*: 1 January 1971 – 31 March 1972, 61.

77. *RWGD*: 1 April 1973 – 31 March 1974, 52.

78. *RWGD*: 1 April 1974 – 31 March 1975, 56.

79. *RWGD*: 1 April 1975 – 31 March 1976, 60.

80. *RWGD*: 1 April 1974 – 31 March 1975, 56; *RWGD*: 1 April 1975 – 31 March 1976, 61.

81. *RWGD*: 1 April 1977 – 31 March 1978, 66.

82. *RWGD*: 1 April 1979 – 31 March 1980, 62.

83. *RWGD*: 1 January – 31 December 1981, 63.

84. *RWGD*: 1 January – 31 December 1983, 61.

85. *RWGD*: 1 January – 31 December 1986, 68.

86. *RWGD*: 1 January – 31 December 1985, 67.

87. *Report on the working of the Museum Department for the year 1970* (Malta, 1972), 7.

88. *RWGD*: 1 April 1977 – 31 March 1978, 64.

89. http://whc.unesco.org/criteria.htm

90. *RWGD*: 1 January – 31 December 1992, 81, 219.

91. 'Cultural Heritage Act 2002', *Supplement to the Government Gazette*, No. 17,232, 26 April 2002, Act VI of 2002.

92. During the last few years the department has been particularly active in participating or organizing international exhibitions. Among the latter one may mention Florence 1996, Prague 1999, San Marino 2001, Brussels 2001, Geneva 2001, Copenhagen 2002, and Stockholm and Helsinki 2003.